How to Relate
To Your Pastor

HOW TO RELATE
TO YOUR PASTOR

Mark T. Barclay

All scripture references are quoted from the
King James Version of the Holy Bible
unless otherwise noted.

Revised Edition
First Printing 1995

ISBN 0-944802-26-5

Write:
Mark Barclay Ministries
P.O. Box 588, Midland, MI 48640-0588

CONTENTS

FOREWORD

JOHN OSTEEN, Pastor
Lakewood International
Houston, Texas

"The book, *How to Relate to Your Pastor*, by Mark T. Barclay, is one that has been long overdue. We believe it will be of great value to the Body of Christ. We hold the author in high esteem and know that God will reward him for this labor of love."

ED DUFRESNE, Prophet
Ed Dufresne Ministries
Southern California

"I certainly recommend *How to Relate to Your Pastor*. It is an excellent book that will help you understand the ministry and the heart of a pastor in a scriptural way."

BOB LEMON, Apostle
Harvest Fire Ministries

"Pastor Barclay has done an outstanding job in his book, *How to Relate to Your Pastor*, teaching us how to relate to our supernatural pastors. It is very important in these last days that God's people understand the office of pastor. As we put into practice these seven steps, the Church will grow in numbers, and it will also increase the Church's vision for the world. Unity is the key to church growth, and this book will produce unity."

GEORGE ERIC EVANS
President/Founder, Berean Bible College
Pastor, Bible Missionary Temple
San Diego, California

"A message for all congregations. This is the book of insights for a closer relationship between pastor and his people. I rate the book as excellent!"

BUDDY BELL, Teacher
Ministry of Helps International
Tulsa, Oklahoma

"*How to Relate to Your Pastor* is one answer to several questions that people have about the church. I believe all laypeople and ministry gifts should read this book thoroughly in order to better the Kingdom of God. This book will enrich your understanding of God's order for the church."

A WORD FROM THE AUTHOR

Since the first printing of *Seven Bible Ways to Properly Relate to Your Pastor*, different ministry friends have come to me, expressing their concern that certain statements in the book were being taken out of context by the critics. Taking their advice on these matters, we have reproofed the book.

You will find that in this revised edition we have reworded some of the statements that seem to be so misunderstood. We are not apologetic in any way for the heart of the matter in this book, for we have written it to cause peace and unity between pastors and their congregations. However, because we have written it to be a help, we want it to be as simple and as easily understood as it possibly can. This is not easy with what is mostly considered a touchy subject.

I have found that the moment you teach on pastor-people relationships or anything on how to relate to your pastor, there are skeptics and critics who immediately categorize you with people who may be in shepherding error. As a matter of fact, in the first edition of this book, *Seven Bible Ways to Properly Relate to Your Pastor*, I had consistent questions presented to me on that very issue because of the way that I worded certain things.

This is not shepherding error or any other kind of virus or strain to Christianity. I, personally, as an author and Bible teacher, am not into shepherding errors, neither do I endorse them.

As you read through this book, please note that we are not exalting any ministry gift in any way, neither are we making the pastor a mediator between God and other believers. If you are submitted to a man who is submitted to Jesus, there should be no scriptural reason why you would not want to obey these seven scriptural ways that I have pointed out in this book.

Please note that this does not exhaust the subject in any way, neither does it give a full description, for this is not a thorough writing or a complete commentary of any sort. This is simply a small book with quick facts, explaining seven scriptures from the Bible and how we can apply them.

There are also, on these pages, illustrations and testimonies of how people (and they are great people—God's people) have encouraged me at different times in my pastoral life. So if you have a heart that is absent of criticism and you're not hunting to defame, you will find that the heart of the author on these pages is simply to encourage believers to have respect, esteem, and love in the way that they deal with, speak to, speak about, and relate to the pastor who is watching over their soul.

We must take into consideration when we read a small article like this that there are many believers who are troubled, and therefore they will not like the writings on these pages. We also must take into consideration that there are pastors who do defraud, and there are pastors who live in violation of the Holy Scriptures, but certainly you understand that you should not be submitted to such people to begin with. I highly recommend to you to sit under a righteous man's ministry.

I encourage you to read through the entire writing and be encouraged by it and not take any of its individual statements out of context, neither overemphasize the heart of the author.

God bless you as you study and read this book. Let it inspire you and enhance you to be a better Christian, and let lawlessness be found nowhere in your life. My prayer is that both you and your pastor will live right and be clean and that you will build a wonderful, Christ-like working relationship to preach the gospel as a team.

INTRODUCTION

The Lord taught me some very positive things about how to pastor supernaturally, and that's what I want. Don't you want your pastor to be supernatural? I just believed God on how to do things supernaturally, and do you know what I found out? As I received those things and started putting them into operation, as I tried to get out of my mind the background of traditions and ideas of what I was supposed to be as a pastor, and as I listened to the Holy Spirit, something happened—and it wasn't what I expected.

I wanted everything to flow and be productive, but as I started to look at some of my prime workers and ministers in the church, I saw that they were frustrated. They were having trouble getting things done. Well, that sort of bothers you if you're the pastor and you know that they are good people. You know from their past performance that they know what they are doing and that they hear from the Lord. They have been with you long enough that you have confidence in their ministry, which I did, but I started to see them become frustrated. It wouldn't flow anymore for some reason. So I went to the Lord.

I began to really examine the situation, and as I observed, I found that God's people did not know how to relate to me any longer. I had shifted gears on them. I began to think and do things supernaturally, and they no longer knew how to relate to that kind of pastor. They were used to me being the typical "follow the format and guide-book" pastor.

You know, a pastor can get frustrated really quickly if everyone around him is frustrated. If the jobs aren't getting done, people aren't getting saved, there's no healing, and the anointing is all bottled up, it can become a real problem—and does!

I started hearing things throughout the local church—little murmurs, little baaaaas from the sheep. They were frustrated because they did not really know how to relate to the shepherd. Then one got bold enough to come to me and say, "I love you so much, Pastor, and I love you as a man of God, and I want to do what is right. I want to do this [what you teach us]. I know it's the Bible. You open the Bible and you teach us, but for some reason, it's not working for me. I don't know what to do." They'd say things like, "I used to go to a denominational church. I went to a church that was different than this. The pastor spent all of his time going from home to home and counseling, and he didn't teach us the things you are teaching us. He didn't expect us to do anything. There was no demand on our lives. And now, all of a sudden, we are here [from that certain fellowship, church, or denomination] in this local church, and every-thing is different. I don't understand why you do this, and I don't understand why the ushers do that. Please teach me how to relate to you. I love you and Vickie so much, and I want to be a part of this ministry. I want to do what's right. I want to love you. I want to be able to communicate with you. I want to see in the Bible the right way to treat my pastor."

Do you know what I said? "Um, um, well, golly gee, I

don't know what to say." In my heart I was determined to find out because I was more disoriented about this than he was. I didn't know what to say. I knew what I was doing, only because I would go to my prayer closet, open the Bible, and the Holy Ghost would say, "Go do this." I'd go do it, and after I was done, I was back to the Lord for help. So I began to seek God and His Word for wisdom on this matter. "Father, now you put sheep in the house of the Lord, and you have told me to be a good shepherd. Some of the things I am to do are corral them, protect them, teach them, and feed them. So please show me in the Bible something that will feed Your people and give them avenues that will allow them to relate to Vickie and me as their pastors and, in turn, serve You more effectively."

The Lord showed it to me for the local church. As I taught this message to the church, people would come and say, "We have never seen anything like that before. No one has ever taught us this." Let me ask you, reader, in your heart, right now, would you like to relate to your pastor? Would you like to know him and his wife? You see, everyone wants to relate to their pastor. You women of the church, don't you want to relate to your pastor and his wife? Get in there, and get something to "hold on to." Get to know them. Well, you know, a pastor can rattle his brains out, spend his life trying to relate to you, and if you don't know how to relate in return, there is blockage. Where there is blockage, little anointing flows. Where little anointing flows, there are still yokes and bondages. Under these conditions, things just aren't the best.

Some of you pastors—you need to hear this. You are going to be frustrated until you get people to relate to you and work with you—supernaturally. You have to train them to do the work. You have to equip them to relate to you and work with you. Believe it or not, they want to work, and they want to relate, but in most cases, they need a leader.

Now it needs to be said (before you read this book) that these are Bible ways to relate to your pastor. They are not only Barclay ways, and they are not only nondenominational ways. It needs to be understood that they are Bible ways. As you read this book, you will see that only the Bible is used for reference and support of what is being taught.

I ask you to see the heart of this matter and not just the fringes of it. Please don't take statements out of context or exaggerate these seven points. My intentions are to stir you to build better partnerships and deeper working relationships.

CHAPTER 1
HOW TO RECEIVE YOUR PASTOR
AS A GIFT

"Wherefore he saith, When he ascended up on high, he led captivity captive, and gave gifts unto men."

Ephesians 4:8

Jesus is he who has ascended. This scripture tells us that Jesus gave gifts unto men. Let's examine the next scripture to see what these gifts are.

"And he gave some, apostles; and some, prophets; and some, evangelists; and some, pastors and teachers ..."

Ephesians 4:11

Who gave these gifts? Jesus. To whom did He give them? Us. Okay, let's look even further to see why He gave us these ministry gifts.

"For the perfecting of the saints, for the work of the ministry, for the edifying of the body of Christ ..."

Ephesians 4:12

Let's make sure we understand exactly what is being said. From whom did apostles, prophets, evangelists, pastors, and teachers come? God. Who gave them to us? Jesus. To whom did He give these gifts? The church.

1

Okay, Church, I ask you this simple, biblical question: How did we get these apostles, prophets, evangelists, pastors, and teachers? Did we buy them? No. If we didn't buy them, do we have to pay for them? No. Did we steal them? No. If we didn't steal them, we don't have to hide them. How did we get them? They were given to us, and if they were given to us, they were and are gifts. Sure, the heavenly gift is in them, but they must be a vessel God endorses or why would He gift them?

One pastor asked, "Brother Barclay, you taught this in your own church?" I said, "That's right, because it's just as much truth as anything else, and just between you and me, pastor, I needed to teach this in my church as much as any truth." Apostles, prophets, evangelists, pastors, and teachers are gifts from Jesus! We need to get this in us. I know we probably have heard it ten thousand times, but even so, they are gifts. I tell you one thing, we had better not abuse them because God gave them to us.

Examine this illustration with me. Let's say I wanted to give you something, and I decided it was to be a $100 bill. So I take my wallet out, I sort through the bills, and I find one that I want to give away. I say, "Hey you, I am going to give you this $100 bill." You say, "Oh glory, glory, glory. I have been believing for $100. Only God knew that I needed $100." But I still have the $100 bill, and you are still standing there jumping up and down. I still have the $100 bill. Can you see it? Just knowing this $100 is yours is not enough. It will do you no good until you receive it. The same is true with your pastor. So the first Bible way to relate to your pastor is to receive him. It's not enough that God gave him to us; we have to receive him.

Let me tell you churches, teaching centers, and revival

centers of today—you have got to receive him. All of these are full of people who want something. They're seeking to get it, and when it's laid out before them, many won't receive it.

I remember when I first came to Midland. No one invited me here, and not too many were excited that I came. But I came, obedient to the Holy Ghost. He told me to come.

As people came in, they began to tell me they had believed that I was the right man for this area. Oh, you should've heard the stories. They would say things like, "We were in the pits before you came, and now it's going to be okay." They would come in and shout and stomp a few times, but the first time they heard the Word—man, they split. They didn't receive me. They said, "Oh, you great gift from the Lord; we are just so thankful you came into this area. Praise the Lord." But they never received me as their pastor. There are people going to the church now who still haven't received me. Many have, but many haven't.

Every church has people in attendance who consider it their home church but don't consider the pastor their pastor. Others consider the man as their pastor but not the church as their church. Many tithe elsewhere, and some tithe not at all. Strange, isn't it?

There are people going to their local churches, and if you ask them why they are going to that church, they'll say things like, "Well, it's the only thing around." Well, now that really encourages your pastor. We are glad you're here because there is just nowhere else to go. These people don't recognize their pastor as a ministry gift. They don't recognize him as one gifted by the Lord.

Do you know who they have recognized as a pastor? They run down to Brother Evangelist's meeting and say, "Ooooooh and Aaaaaah. Pastor Prophet, Pastor Teacher, Pastor Evangelist, Pastor Apostle." Now, you have never heard these men say that they were a pastor. If we would just listen, we would hear them say what they are—apostle, prophet, evangelist, or teacher. In fact, if you listen closely, they'll tell you to be fed, taught, and disciplined in a local church. These men are definitely doing something wonderful for Jesus, but they are not your pastor. When they come to town, we pass the word. We get as many of you in their meetings as we can because we want you to hear what that ministry gift has to say. It will change your life and change your church. That is why God called them. However, they're not your pastor.

People sit in church, and they come to the pastor, and they want him to teach their children, counsel their marriage, teach them the Bible, and be here every Sunday because they have nowhere else to go. Yet the moment that Brother Evangelist is in town, they've got to go. They've got to go to him.

Have you ever noticed that as soon as it is time to take the offering in the local church, people get out their little offering card, and they get out their little list of whom they give to, and many times, local churches are on the bottom of the list.

If you were to ask them why they haven't tithed here lately, they would tell you something like, "Well, the Lord spoke to me to give to Brother Prophet two years ago." Are you listening? I hope you understand. I give to all those ministries too. I love them. I thank God for them. They are as much a ministry gift as the office of pastor. We all should get behind them and push them—financially, spiritually, and every other way. They are doing something for God . . . maybe something big for God. My point is, until you settle down in a local church and receive your pastor as a ministry gift, you are hurting and robbing yourself.

I tell you, it's time not to be children anymore, tossed to and fro by every little wind of doctrine and every little snarl, bicker, and complaint. It's time to rise up and say, "I have a leader; I have a pastor. He's looking after my soul, and I submit to him. He is a gift from Jesus (the Son of the Living God), and I receive him. He's mine. I receive him. He's mine." Now, that's the Bible! I tell you, I've received my pastor, and he's not even here. I pastor a local church, but I have a pastor, and I love him very much. Do you know what I do for my pastor? I send him money, I call him on the phone occasionally, I write him letters, and never once have I ever told my pastor a complaint. Never once have I ever said anything that was not good about his ministry. This is not shepherdship error, this is being mature. I try to be a blessing, not dump on him all the time.

I am a child of God. I am a believer. I would never make my pastor's life miserable. He's my gift. Praise God. I have received him. He's mine because I have received him. You cannot relate to your pastor properly until you have thoroughly, in your heart, made him your pastor.

If a gift comes in a box, and it looks all nice and pretty, all concealed, and you're just itching to see what's in there, you want to enjoy it and get everything out of it that you can—forget it until you open that box. You can say, "Oh, that's my gift. Isn't that nice?" But you have to open it. You can say, "It's mine, and I'll open it if I want to." That's fine, but until you do, you won't enjoy or thoroughly understand and use the gift. You'll always be guessing and wondering.

Oh, saints of God—receive your pastor. Go to Jesus and voice to him that you receive the gift He's given you. (Now, you understand that the apostle, prophet, evangelist, and teacher are also very vital gifts, and we need to relate to them also. I am concentrating on the office of pastor in this book, and that is why we emphasize it here the most.)

We need to go to our pastor and voice to him that we receive him as a gift of the Lord and then begin to relate to him accordingly.

Before we close this chapter of the book and enter into Bible Way #2, we should consider one more thing. Let's look together at this next scripture.

> *"Ye also, as lively stones, are built up a spiritual house . . ."*
>
> 1 Peter 2:5

Another translation says that we are "being built into a spiritual house." This is what God is doing in the Church today.

If you are one who will submit to and relate to your pastor spiritually, then you will reap from his ministry spiritual things. If you are one who will submit to and relate to your pastor only in a natural or religious way, you will probably reap mostly natural things. You will seldom see or draw from the Jesus in him because you are looking at his personality, style, or looks, and therefore you may not recognize the spiritual.

It is more than fair to mention here that some pastors

live wrong or have never developed their character. In 2 Timothy 3:10 we are taught to follow doctrine, manner of life, etc. Please be sure you are submitting yourself to a pastor with godly character and lifestyle.

None of us should look beyond sin, but we can look beyond styles, systems, prejudices, personalities, and personal preferences in order to tap into the gift and anointing.

Now, agree with me that spiritual doesn't mean spooky. Many folks think that if they have feelings, goose bumps, and emotional warmth that they are spiritual. If they have to do something with their hands or work in any way, then that is carnal and not quite so spiritual. What a major misunderstanding!

Sad to say, it shows in the Body of Christ today. If you are submitted to your pastor supernaturally, then it doesn't bother you when he makes a mistake. Why? Because you are seeing the office of pastor, and you're looking at the God in him. You don't excuse or totally ignore the mistake, but you have confidence in God that Jesus is big enough to deal with it. (By the way, mistakes aren't always sin. Immorality and other sins should cause you to reconsider your commitment to that particular ministry.)

CHAPTER 2
HOW TO KNOW YOUR PASTOR
AND HIS WIFE

"And we beseech you, brethren, to know them which labour among you, and are over you in the Lord . . ."

1 Thessalonians 5:12

What does it say to do? To know those who labor among you and are over you in the Lord. Your pastor, who labors among you, is a man of God and has authority, and he's looking out for your soul. Perhaps you're not used to that. Perhaps you're used to hearing, "Pastor, do this, and Pastor, do that. Pastor, please, Pastor, visit me because I missed a Sunday service." When you get under a supernatural man of God, he's not playing those games. He means business. He's hearing from God, and if you are, you'll get blessed.

Let me illustrate. The congregation just loves their pastor, and he stands at the door after each service, and they say, "Bless you, bless you, good sermon, bless you, bless you." But the minute that he becomes the one who is over you in the Lord, it's a different story. It now is heard, "What right does he have to teach that kind of stuff? Well, who does he think he is? Well, it wasn't like this at the church that I came from."

Now let's look at more of the scripture.

"And we beseech you, brethren, to know them which labour among you, and are over you in the Lord, and admonish you . . ."

Now, this cuts out the less mature really quick. ". . . Admonish you!" Have you ever heard this? "Now, you know that we can take a little authority; we'll go along with that. He's Pastor. But he had better not talk to me like he just talked to Brother So-and-so."

Sometimes people go around the church and say, "You know Brother So-and-so. He's the one coordinating the church services here, and he's giving orders and everything. Man, I sure wish I had his job. He doesn't have anything to do but go around telling everyone else what to do." Well, it would be nice if the same person who mouthed all this criticism happened to be in the office when Pastor disciplined Brother So-and-so or corrected him for something he did not do that he was supposed to do. Do you know what Brother So-and-so did when he was corrected by pastor? He is a mature person. He didn't quit. He didn't curse. He didn't cry. He didn't pout. He said, "Yes, sir. It'll never happen again." Do you know what? It never happened again, and he's still getting everything done—even better than before. The Pastor doesn't have to babysit him nearly as much. So what if your pastor admonishes you! You should ask him to. It will keep you straight.

You see, we must know him. Some people would like to take the pastor out to supper. That would be okay, but that's not what it means to know him. It's much deeper than that. "Well, Brother Glenn is always with the pastor, but I never get to be with him." It didn't say to have the pastor babysit you. It said to know those who labor among you and are over you and admonish you. How do you know him? Study him. How do you find out something? How do you know something? You study! Know him. Watch him. Watch him, study him, and take notes on him (not that he is the standard, but he is supposed to be leading by example). Relationship is the key here. The more you know a person, the better you can relate. It helps to know one's character if you plan to walk together. The less you know a person, the more difficult it is to understand him.

"Well, he's not my God. I'm following Jesus!" Not like you should be if you're not following your pastor as he follows Jesus. If you don't know your pastor and you're not going to put any effort into knowing him, then forget it. You may never walk in the fullness of what God has for you because your pastor's the one whom God has put in your life to flow with God's anointing to help you. He is not the mediator between you and God. You have an anointing in you from no man. Even so, God gave us gifts to perfect us and equip us. If you are in a place where there is no pastor at all, pray fervently. You are missing out on some wonderful things.

We see in the Book of Acts that it was the apostles whom God sent from the church. The Holy Ghost spoke to the gathering of believers and said, ". . . separate unto me . . ." Now don't get the itch and split. Stick around and work, and maybe someday the Lord will say, "Why don't you separate So-and-so for the work that I have called them to, let the anointing flow on their life, send them out of there, and support them as they go." Now that's Bible, and you're not going to do that until you know your pastor and he knows you. "Well, I don't know, if he'd just let me come over once in a while. He never lets me come over, and I try to call him but no luck." One brother called, and was he hot. He called and got an answering machine, and the next time his pastor saw him, he came up and said, "I'll tell you something right now. When I call my pastor, I like to get ahold of him." Well, you know, that's really sad. He said, "How do you expect me to get to know you if I can't ever get you on the phone to tell you all my problems, to have you solve them for me, and have you help me out? If I don't spend time with you, how am I going to get to know you?"

Study, man. Study! For some reason, we go through school cheating. You know, in high school you do okay in some grades, but then you get car-crazy, girl-crazy, and all other crazy things. Then, studying just isn't the focus of your attention for a while. So you go to cheating—looking at what the neighbor has, taking down the wrong notes, bribing, conniving, and cheating—getting lazy. We just kind of grow up that way. We come in the church, and we are lazy. We don't want to settle down in the local church, be disciplined, study the man of God, watch how he handles hard situations, and watch how the anointing comes on his life. Do you know why many don't want to do that? Because they have never received him. If they had received him, they would be watching that man and saying, "Would you make that move again? I missed a couple of things in the way you handled that tough situation. I am trying to learn from your example, and I missed something you did in that last maneuver. How did you win that victory?"

You need to understand that your pastor isn't your god, nor is he your savior, and he isn't wanting you to worship him. But, if he's a man of God and if he is your pastor, relate to him properly and biblically. This will benefit you as well as him.

One day, prior to service, a couple of ushers were in my office when I dealt with a man in a bad spirit. Well, it was a really bad situation, and this man was giving us a hard time. As far as I was concerned, he was being used of the devil and was acting like a thief. Boy, he just ranted and raved and told me the way it was going to be. I let him go for a while (trying to understand him), and he began to get a little carried away. He threatened to publicly harass and interrupt our meeting. I was kind of looking at the other men in the office, and I wondered what they would do if I just walked out of the room. (Doth the Lord always speak through Moses?) That would have been one time I would like to have said, "You handle it, ushers," and walked out. I had to use some Holy Ghost boldness and rebuke that man and set him in his place with the Word of the Lord. Then I told an usher, "If he wants to stay, take him to the back of the church, sit him down, and if he so much as sneezes, you haul him out. As long as he sits and behaves (I wanted him to hear this), he can worship, he can learn, he can love; but if he does anything out of order, you grab him and haul him out of here."

The church didn't know about this, but the ushers did their job well because they had received their pastor, and they had confidence in his judgment and in his hearing from the Holy Ghost. They watched a rough situation and learned. Watch how your pastor deals with these kinds of things.

Now, some of you say, "I sure would like to have time to study the pastor and have time to be with the pastor, but I don't." Well, go to church! Take notes. Study. A lot of pastors are not going to tell you that, because when you start taking notes, you see the good and the bad. You see both the strong points as well as weak ones. Pastors aren't perfect. Don't be fooled. You should follow the Christ-like attributes that you see in them. He is not your god, and he shouldn't lord over you. But he is going to pastor you, and as long as you receive him, you'll receive tremendous aid in your Christian life.

If you'll just sit down and take time to know your pastor, it will change your life. You know, you can even learn from your pastor's personal life. He is your example! How does he act when he is not behind the pulpit? How does he overcome attacks on his life and family? How does he keep the victory?

CHAPTER 3
HOW TO ESTEEM HIM
HIGHLY IN LOVE

"And to esteem them very highly in love for their work's sake. And be at peace among yourselves."

1 Thessalonians 5:13

Esteem here does not mean to exalt. We exalt Jesus; we esteem and honor our leadership.

We need to take a good look at this. Does it say to esteem them sort of highly? No. To esteem them highly? No. To esteem them very highly? Yes.

Not a lot of pastors would teach you this, would they? But it is as much Bible as anything else. Some people don't want to hear this kind of teaching because it places responsibility on them. They say, "That's not the way I believe. Don't tell me that stuff." Many are so inoculated with the devil's suspicion that they are paranoid of leadership. "What if it's shepherding error or cultish leadership or a spirit of control?" they say. Admit it or not, there are people like this in the Body of Christ. Even so, let's obey the Bible and esteem our pastor very highly in love—not in pride, not in an arrogant way, not bowing down like he is your God. Esteem him very highly in love. Why? Because he's good looking? No. Because you like the suit he wears?

No. Because you like the way he combs his hair? No. Because you like his new car? No. Why? For his work's sake. Don't be one who says, "Brother Barclay, I would like to esteem my pastor highly like you esteem yours, but well, ah, well, ah, he just doesn't do so well sometimes. I don't get fed. I just lost my respect for him." No one said to esteem him highly for who he is or how he's doing. It said for his work's sake. What is his work? Pastoring. Even if your pastor is troubled, your love and care toward him will be an encouragement to bring him through. Don't give up on him. Help him get help.

You esteem him very highly because Jesus made him your pastor. There are things that will bless him—just little things (for example: being polite, causing unity, and being sweet).

Let me share an illustration. I had this football coach in high school, and I admired him. He wasn't only a good coach, he was a good football player. We had a good team. One day I went into his office. I was a cocky teenager, and I called him by his last name, "Hey, (and then his last name)." That guy came out of that chair and slapped me a good one. That taught me something as a young man. Whatever your title is, I shall call you that. So when I am around pastors, I don't say, "Hi, ya, there, old buddy. How ya doin?" He's not an old buddy. He's a pastor. Well, is he your pastor? No, but it is still his work. He is still a gift. Jesus still gave him. He is a pastor. This is not a law. You do not have to do this. I am not teaching you to overemphasize a man's title but rather to show some simple respect. It isn't so important that you use the term as it is that you show some respect and honor. You have to esteem pastors very highly in love for their work's sake in order to fulfill the Word of God.

Now, your pastor is not going to enjoy you being around if you're calling him "old Joe," tripping over his shoes, throwing his coat on the floor, slamming the car door in his face, and talking your street slang. For someone who lives in the Spirit of God, that bothers or quenches them. But when you begin to show courtesy, like putting his coat on for him or opening the car door for him and treating him as a man of God, it's going to say something to him. The next time he needs some company or a driver or some help, he's going to say, "I know who treats the ministry gift properly. I'll just call up Brother So-and-so, and he'll go with me. He'll do it right." Some people today are getting an itch to go. They want to go. Well, learn how to go. Then your leader will say in his heart, "I know who I can take with me that will know how to act in this certain situation and in this meeting. He'll act professionally, he'll keep his mouth shut about what he hears, he'll be on time, and he will be a help in the fulfillment of this mission."

How else can I esteem my pastor very highly in love for his work's sake? Probably the greatest way is with your mouth. Many people eat up and spit out their pastor every day. They judge and give poor confessions over his teachings and actions, especially disciplinary actions. Begin to say good things about your pastor and his family. Also, don't lower yourself to listen to others when they are being unscriptural in their speech toward their pastor.

God will bless you and honor you as you walk in integrity and love, even if others don't. There has seldom, if ever, been a church split where everyone loved and esteemed their pastor—quite the contrary. Peace leaves when esteem leaves. Look again at 1 Thessalonians 5:13.

CHAPTER 4
HOW TO PRAY FOR HIM

"Finally, brethren, pray for us, that the word of the Lord may have free course, and be glorified, even as it is with you . . ."

2 Thessalonians 3:1

Why should we pray for our pastor? So that the Word of the Lord will have free course. Don't pray this: "Oh, Father, I see the problem my pastor has, bless him, bless him, bless him. He is so poor. I want him to have so much blessing. Bless him, bless him." You know that you should pray he'll be blessed, but you should not pray in that attitude. The motivation causing you to pray for your pastor should be the scripture telling us that the Word will have free course. (If your pastor is really in sin, then pray even more fervently that God will intervene. Do your best to try to help him.)

God said that you pay your tithe so there'll be meat in His house. What is meat? Is it lightbulbs, pews, carpeting? No, no. It's the Word! Who brings you the Word? Mostly the pastor. Why do we pray for him? So the Word will have free course. That means if you don't pay your tithe and don't pray for him, you have just bottled up the Word, and it's not as much Pastor's responsibility as it is yours. If the city is not being won, the Word is not going forth with power, and there are no signs and wonders and miracles, it may be because you and others have quit doing your part. Let's do our part, and while we are, pray for our pastors that the Word will have free course and be glorified, just like it is for you.

Wouldn't it be a shame if we all just came to church and danced, shouted, and worshipped the Lord, but never told anyone? Wouldn't it be something if we all came into the sanctuary and the pastor stood up to the pulpit and told us that we needed meat in the house today and that we needed to hear directly from the Holy Ghost. But after this brief announcement, he leaves the pulpit and comes down to seat himself in the front row. Now, all of us are looking at the pulpit, waiting for meat. We are waiting to hear from the Holy Spirit. Now, wouldn't that be silly? You see, God uses the ministry gifts to minister to us from His Word as the Head of the Church directs us. Yes, the real teacher, the Holy Spirit, will speak through our pastor and even more so when we pray properly for him.

Also, you and I realize that there are some men and women who call themselves pastors, but Jesus (the Head of the Church) never appointed them, and it is obvious. Pray for them especially.

Let me share with you this testimony. One day in our business office, my wife was praying and asking the Lord for help. We had an important appointment that evening, which we had scheduled well in advance. Our babysitter called and had to cancel on us. We had called around to some of our substitute sitters, but everyone seemed to be busy. My wife sat back in her chair and spoke briefly to the Lord. She explained the importance of the appointment and the problem she was having with a babysitter. As she was talking to the Lord, the phone rang. It was one of the sweet ladies who attended our church. She told my wife how she had just then been praying for us, and the Lord put it in her heart to babysit for us. So . . . she was calling to see if we needed something as silly as a babysitter. Oh boy, did we ever! Was this a life or death matter? Not for us, but maybe for those who were ministered to that evening. Just think about it for a moment. This little lady will have a great part in the rewards of the meeting we had that night.

Listen to this testimony. At a meeting where I was teaching, one of the people there slipped me a note in an envelope. I had placed it in my pocket until I could read it privately. I had forgotten about the envelope until I got home. When I took it out and read the note (which truly was encouraging and a blessing in itself), there was also a check enclosed for over $4000. The next morning I was speaking to a brother in a restaurant. He said, "Pastor, I've been fasting and praying for your personal finances for the past few days. I just want to know if anything has come in. I asked the Lord this morning that He would show me some fruit of my prayers for you." When I told him of the $4000 check that was given to me, we both had a "shout down" right there in the restaurant.

Praise God for saints who care enough and are serious enough to pray for their pastor. All Christian leaders are under severe attack today. They need believers like never before to pray and believe God. We all want to be effective and to help lost, sick, and suffering humanity. This is not done effectively without prayer. Pray for your pastor that he would be delivered from wicked and unreasonable men (1 Thess. 3:2).

CHAPTER 5
HOW TO COMMUNICATE TO HIM

"Let him that is taught in the word communicate unto him that teacheth in all good things."

Galatians 6:6

We should realize here that the Bible says to communicate. This doesn't necessarily say tithe. Tithe is the first-fruits of your income, and according to the Bible, it is expected of us to give Him this "one-tenth" first. (Read Hebrews 7:5 and Galatians 3:7.)

Here is Galatians 6:6 from the Amplified Bible:

"Let him who receives instruction in the Word [of God] share all good things with his teacher [contributing to his support]."

I have found that many people bow their head between their elbows and grit their teeth whenever preachers use two words. The first one is work. When a pastor begins to inform the people that they are to work, the men are separated from the boys. In most churches, the pastor does all this work, and that's what he's paid to do, so why should people interfere? Isn't that sad? The second word is more scoffed at than the first. The word is money. I wonder if we could even count high enough to accurately register all the quarrels, hurt feelings, and church splits that have happened over money, the use of it, or the control of it.

I believe the Bible very simply and clearly shows us that we are to work for the Lord and give of our financial substance. In fact, the Word of the Lord tells us that "where your treasure is, there will your heart be also." I don't know about you, friend, but both my money and my heart are in the spreading of the gospel.

"Well, Brother Barclay, what can I do to bless my pastor and fulfill Galatians 6:6?" Please allow me to share with you a couple of testimonies and then a few avenues for you to take.

When I first came to Midland, Michigan, I was driving a nice new car. No church had invited us here, so no church was paying us a salary. We moved simply in obedience to God's Word. After we arrived, we settled and began making plans for this new church that God had directed us to pastor. At this date, no one in Midland knew us. Vickie and I were determined to fulfill the vision and the direction that God had given us. We put everything we had into the ministry. We had also decided to sell our car to relieve us of payments and allow us more freedom financially. In turn, we found an old, rusted-out, beat-up, oil-burning Ford. Now, the fact that it was a Ford was the only good point about the car. Everything else was rather critical in its operation. In fact, in the spring, as I drove around town, people must have thought I was fogging mosquitoes. There was a hole in the muffler and also the floorboard, so whenever the thing ran, it would pump exhaust right into the car. (Just for the record, I had not taken a poverty oath, neither was I enjoying any of this.) As the church grew, the Lord sent believers who meant business with Him and who were givers. Thank God! A beautiful friend of mine came up to me one day and said, "You're my pastor, and my pastor is not going to drive that thing that you are driving any longer. I have a new car that I am going to pay off and bless you with." He said it would take him a few weeks to pay it off and get everything ready. The next time I saw him and his pretty wife, they said, "The Lord told us you needed a car now, not a few weeks from now." They gave it . . . I received it. As I look back over this, I really don't remember who was more blessed—them for giving or me for receiving. Both of us sure grinned big that day.

Let me share with you about my truckload of beans. One of the farmers in our church family decided to give me a whole truckload of beans at harvesttime. He wanted to invite me out and have the truck driven up to me and say, "Here, Pastor, I want you to have a truckload of beans." Well, it never seemed to work out just the way he wanted, but he was still going to give me those beans. One evening after service I was handed a small envelope from this family. I slipped it in my pocket and had forgotten about it until I got home and began to empty my pockets. I opened that little envelope and read the note and looked at that check for over $4000, and it moved me tremendously. These people were giving to their pastor so that he could give himself to the ministry and the church work rather than secular work.

Another time as I was leaving church after a service, a gentleman, who is a strong member of the church, came up to me and asked if I had a stereo. I said, "No, not yet." He said, "Okay," and walked away. I had forgotten about this little conversation until I was returning home from dinner that same day. This same brother was napping in his van in front of our house. Do you know what he was doing? He came to give me his stereo equipment. When he arrived at my home, I was not there. He was determined to do this, so he waited most of the afternoon until we returned home. Do you know what he said? "I love you, Pastor. This stereo meant a whole lot to me, and there is not another person I would rather have it than you." I could have lived without that stereo, but it is hard to put in words what that did for me personally. That brother's love and giving encouraged me so.

One of the greatest ways for us to relate to our pastor is to give him some of our time. Most pastors study, pray, and prepare for hours each week in order to bless and teach us in church services. Your pastor is totally blessed when he looks over the congregation and sees your face. Your pastor is slightly sorrowed when he looks, and you're not there. Bless him, bless the Lord, and bless yourself . . . be there!

Let me share with you these following avenues to bless your pastor. It is very proper for one of the associates or elders of the church to receive an offering from the saints for the pastor's wedding anniversary, birthday, and for Christmas. It is well in order to give to your pastor just out of appreciation. Did you ever think of sending them a little card or note to encourage them? Maybe your pastor would accept an invitation to go out to dinner with you and be able to relax. These are suggestions that will help you bless your pastor and relate to him. If you'll ask the Lord to show you, he will reveal to you even greater ways to help, bless, and relate to your pastor.

Of course, giving to the local church work and tithing are at the top of the list. It relieves tons of pressure off of your pastor when the church bills can be paid on time and the projects come to completion.

CHAPTER 6
HOW TO FOLLOW HIM

"That ye be not slothful, but followers of them who through faith and patience inherit the promises."

Hebrews 6:12

"In order that you may not grow disinterested and become [spiritual] sluggards, but imitators, behaving as do those who through faith (by their leaning of the entire personality on God in Christ in absolute trust and confidence in His power, wisdom, and goodness) and by practice of patient endurance and waiting are [now] inheriting the promises."

Hebrews 6:12 (AMP.)

Notice it says to follow them, and the Amplified here says to imitate them. Many people think it is wrong to copy someone—but it really isn't. Listen to what the great Apostle Paul says:

"Those things, which ye have both learned, and received, and heard, and seen in me, do: and the God of peace shall be with you."

Philippians 4:9

"Practice what you have learned and received and heard and seen in me, and model your way of living

on it, and the God of peace (of untroubled, undis-
turbed well-being) will be with you."

Philippians 4:9 (AMP.)

Paul is saying, in other words, Hey, you can imitate me, the way I follow Christ. You can copy me. Do you want to inherit the promises? Then be an imitator of those who are doing it. Imitate. You know, some people get the itch to go preach. They badly want to go. Well, we want you to go. That's what it's all about, but we want you to go supernaturally, not in the flesh and not overzealously.

Remember when the farm boy Elisha was working in the field, and the prophet of the Lord came around and threw his mantle on him? Most people know this story very well. Elisha went home, did his duties, and then caught up with the prophet and said, I'm sticking close to you, sir, and every once in a while the prophet would say, I'm going over there, and you stay here. The farm boy would say, Forget it, sir. Where you go, you'll see my face. (This Elisha was indeed determined.) A little while later the prophet would say, The Lord has told me to go over there, and you stay here. Not a chance, Elisha would say, I am hooked up. If you go there, I go there. You could say that Elijah became a father-like one or a pastor-like one to Elisha.

Elijah and Elisha had come to Bethel where the sons of the prophets were. These men approached Elisha and began to voice to him that his master was going to leave him this day. Elisha kept his mind stayed on what he was doing for the Lord and told the sons of the prophets to hold their peace. Elijah told Elisha that he was going to cross over to Jericho and that Elisha was to stay in Bethel. As usual, Elisha told his master that he would follow along in order to help. (Can't you just see this today? Here is one man following another man around, running errands, washing his hands, being a servant. The religious crowd made fun of him. I suppose they teased him about being a tagalong and being the pastor's pet.)

Everyone knows the story. Elijah asked Elisha what he wanted, and he said, "A double portion." What happened? Elijah was caught away in a fiery chariot in a whirlwind and dropped his mantle to the ground as he went. Elisha immediately tore off his own clothes and put on the mantle of Elijah. What's the first thing the farm boy (Elisha) did? Did he run off to Bible college to become a preacher? Did he quit and go home because he had lost his leader? Did he run right out and start a church based on what he had seen? No. No. No. Here's what he did. He put on his leader's cloak, and he started back to Bethel where the sons of the prophets were. As he journeyed, he came to the same water that he and his master had come to on the way over. Elisha, knowing that he was now the new anointed leader, smote those waters and said, "Where is the God named Jehovah?" No. No. It didn't happen that way! Elisha came to those waters, and he smote them and said, "Part in the name of Jesus." No. No. That's not the way it happened. Here's how it happened. Elisha came to those waters, and he could see that the sons of the prophets were watching from the other side. They could tell that his leader was not with him. Elisha probably thought a moment and remembered what his pastor would do. He carefully and exactly wrapped that mantle on his hand, just like his pastor did. He carefully and exactly positioned his feet, just like his pastor once did. He reared back and smote those waters exactly like his pastor did, and the sons of the prophets heard him say, "Where is the Lord God of Elijah?" Who? The Lord God of Elijah! Whose God? The Lord God of Elijah! Can you see it? Elisha knew the God of his pastor.

Now we understand that he was also the God of Elisha, and He is still our God today. Praise Him for that! You see, Elisha knew a tremendous truth. As long as he was with his leader, or pastor (Elijah), he was totally submissive, and when his pastor was gone, he knew to imitate him carefully (according to the way he followed God). Elisha smote those waters of Jordan and said, Where is the Lord God of my pastor? Did you see that! What beauty. What truth. What spiritual understanding this man Elisha had—and what results! Those waters parted, Elisha came across, and guess what happened. The sons of the prophets who were a little envious and teased about how submissive Elisha was to his pastor saw this act of authority, heard the words spoken, and came to meet him. They said, "The spirit of Elijah doth rest on Elisha." The Bible says in 2 Kings 2:15 that they came to meet him and bowed themselves to the ground before him.

Can you see it? Elisha had watched his pastor, and he did the exact same thing. He copied him. He imitated his pastor. Now remember, Elisha asked for a double portion, and according to the Bible, he got exactly that.

Do you want an anointing? Do you want to work in the church? Do you want to preach the gospel? Do you want to reach the world? Do you want to be used of God? Imitate and copy your leader in the Lord. This will aid you tremendously to see by example how things are done. A right heart and a good leader can help you advance properly. Relax! Your pastor isn't God—but he is a man of God.

You know, many people don't like this kind of teaching, even though it can be plainly seen in the Bible. I learned something a long time ago. The people who get mad when you preach on tongues are the ones who don't speak in tongues. The people who are stirred when you teach on casting out demons are the ones who have a problem with a demon. The people who get angry when you teach on tithing are the ones who are not tithing properly. So . . . the ones who get upset about submission and this kind of teaching are the ones who are not submissive to their pastor and do not receive him as a man of God or they have over-submitted to a man in a fleshly manner and have gotten hurt. Look closer at the ministry gift Jesus has set over you in the church. Begin to operate Bible ways to properly relate to them. You will be held accountable for this.

CHAPTER 7
HOW TO OBEY HIS TEACHINGS

"Be ye followers of me, even as I also am of Christ.

Now I praise you, brethren, that ye remember me in all things, and keep the ordinances, as I delivered them to you."

1 Corinthians 11:1-2

I gave you these two scriptures to show you this seventh point. I beseech you, brethren. Listen to what the Spirit of God is going to say on the next few pages. It will establish you and change your lives. It will let you see your pastor in a new way in which you may have never seen him before.

You have to be convinced that your pastor is your pastor. You can't just go to church. You have to be convinced. You have to look at him and say, "That is my pastor. He is from God. He is anointed. He is my pastor. He is my gift from the Lord."

If you don't take heed to do what your pastor teaches you, you could be in real trouble. Many are coming to church and are saying, "Devil, I am making a stand with the believers. I am submitted to my pastor and the local church, so phooey on you." Then they walk out of church and don't do what they've said, and the devil smites them or gets their kids or their money or their health or their peace or anything else he can get. Keep the ordinances—not as you desire; not as your opinions say; no, not according to your preference. Keep the ordinances as your pastor delivered them unto you. Be like the Bereans and search the Scriptures daily. Grab hold of the Bible doctrines taught by your pastor and hang on to them. You should be convinced that he's your pastor and he's hearing from God. You must obey your pastor's teachings—that is, if your pastor teaches the Bible. If he doesn't, why have you sat under him and listened? Any pastor sent of God will be teaching the Bible. You see, people want to relate, but some want to do it carnally. They want a babysitter. They want all your time, attention, and the best position of the church. This is not a Bible way to relate. Now look, I am not just teaching the Barclay ways to relate, nor am I just teaching Living Word International's way to relate. These seven steps are Bible ways to relate to your pastor—your leader in the Lord.

Let's examine another passage of scripture.

"Take heed therefore unto yourselves, and to all the flock, over the which the Holy Ghost hath made you overseers, to feed the church of God, which he hath purchased with his own blood.

For I know this, that after my departing shall grievous wolves enter in among you, not sparing the flock.

Also of your own selves shall men arise, speaking perverse things, to draw away disciples after them.

Therefore watch, and remember, that by the space of three years I ceased not to warn every one night and day with tears.

*And now, brethren, I commend you to God, and to the
word of his grace, which is able to build you up . . ."*

Acts 20:28-32

What did that say? "Take heed therefore unto yourselves, and to all the flock, over the which the Holy Ghost
hath made you overseers." No one invited me to come to
Midland where I pastor. No person or board made me the
pastor. No one hired me. The Holy Ghost said, "You, Barclay, go to Michigan and be an overseer of the church in
Midland." At this time there was no church for me to pastor. Living Word International wasn't born yet.

I was obedient to leave, and God placed me there. I
was placed there as an overseer, whether anyone would
come or not. As long as you are there, you are part of the
flock, and I oversee you. When you go, I'm still overseeing
the flock that's there. You didn't make me pastor. You can't
hire me, and you can't fire me. I tell people this (as I see
the need to explain how the church is governed), "Take
heed to yourself [pastor] and to all the flock over the which
the Holy Ghost hath made you overseers."

Why? "To feed the church of God, which he hath purchased with his own blood." Listen to this part. "For I know
this, that after my departing shall grievous wolves enter in
among you, not sparing the flock." You and I both know
there are wolves who want to get at God's sheep! That's
pretty common, isn't it? But that's not all and perhaps not
the worst.

"Also of your own selves shall men arise, speaking
perverse things, to draw away disciples after them." Any
one person who has not received Pastor as the pastor and
who's not convinced that he is their pastor, could become

more dangerous than a wolf. Most of you see the wolves coming in, but it's those among you who rise up with a better idea, judging the ministry gifts. Look out for and mark those who cause division among you, and avoid them. Ye which are spiritual try to restore those who are overtaken in a fault.

Let's read some more. "Therefore watch, and remember, that by the space of three years I ceased not to warn every one night and day with tears." That's a long time, isn't it? For three years this man had warned his church . . . three years! For three years he warned them. "And now, brethren, I commend you to God, and to the word of his grace, which is able to build you up, and to give you an inheritance among all them which are sanctified." Do you realize how little I would do in the supernatural, as your pastor, if I just ran around to everyone's home to make sure everything was okay—to make sure your feelings weren't hurt and that you agreed with the teachings? I know this would be almost impossible to do and still stay in the ministry of the Word of God and prayer. These things will lead pastors away from their number one ministry (Acts 6:1-6).

The Holy Ghost made me the overseer of this flock to feed and guard. I know the ones who are rising up among us, speaking perverse things, drawing disciples after their own kind. If you are one of these, don't get too excited because it won't be long, and Pastor will sit on you. You are not going to get any disciples out of Christ's Church. You might rise up and speak perverse things till Pastor puts his foot on you. That's rough, I know, but it's the Bible way.

This is what I speak to our congregation often: "If you go to my church, I love you. I am responsible for your soul. I am not your Lord. Don't worship me, but I love you, and I am going to do my job. The Holy Ghost made me your overseer. I am going to commend you to God and His Word that is able to build you up. Those who want to be built up, I will just turn you over to the Word. It will build you up. You come to every meeting and learn the Bible, take a few notes, study them, and the Lord will bless your life." The Lord has told me not to entertain wolves. I'll drive them from the flock so that God's sheep can feed in green pastures and in safety.

Now please say this, "I am not a child of the devil, demons don't own me, and he is not my father. The devil is not my lord, my master, or my teacher. I do not listen to a word of what he says. I do not bow down to him. I don't listen to him. I am not moved by him. When he speaks, I laugh. Jesus is my Lord. He has given me a pastor, and now I know how to relate to him properly."

A WORD OF CONCLUSION

- Receive your pastor.   Jesus gave him as a gift.

- Know your pastor.   Study his lifestyle as a Christian leader.

- Esteem him very highly in love.   Be at peace among yourselves.

- Pray for him.   Word will have free course.

- Communicate to him.   Give to his support.

- Imitate him.   Be faithful to follow.

- Obey his teachings.   Grow in the Lord.

How to Relate to Your Pastor was written to show avenues for you to relate to and help the man of God (pastor). I believe that as you read this book, the Holy Spirit stirred you in many areas and avenues in which you could bless your pastor that I didn't even mention. Be moved by God in these things, and be a blessing. You'll see that it will bring you great contentment and satisfaction as you serve Jesus.

As you serve Jesus—serve him well!

Mark T. Barclay

PRAYER OF SALVATION

YOU CAN BE SAVED FROM ETERNAL DAMNA-TION and get God's help now in this life. All you have to do is humble your heart, believe in Christ's work at Calvary for you, and pray the prayer below.

"Dear Heavenly Father:

I know that I have sinned and fallen short of Your expectations of me. I have come to realize that I cannot run my own life. I do not want to continue the way I've been living, neither do I want to face an eternity of torment and damnation.

I know that the wages of sin is death, but I can be spared from this through the gift of the Lord Jesus Christ. I believe that He died for me, and I receive His provision now. I will not be ashamed of Him, and I will tell all my friends and family members that I have made this wonderful decision.

Dear Lord Jesus:

Come into my heart now and live in me and be my Savior, Master, and Lord. I will do my very best to chase after You and to learn Your ways by submitting to a pastor, reading my Bible, going to a church that preaches about **You**, and keeping sin out of my life.

I also ask You to give me the power to be healed from any sickness and disease and to deliver me from those things that have me bound.

I love You and thank You for having me, and I am eagerly looking forward to a long, beautiful relationship with You."

Books by Mark T. Barclay

Beware of Seducing Spirits

This is not a book on demonology. It is a book about the misbehavior of men and women and the seducing/deceiving spirits that influence them to do what they do. Brother Barclay exposes the most prominent seducing spirits of the last days.

Beware of the Sin of Familiarity

This book is a scriptural study on the most devastating sin in the body of Christ today. The truths in this book will make you aware of this excess familiarity and reveal to you some counterattacks.

Building a Supernatural Church

A guide to pioneering, organizing, and establishing a new local church. This is a fast-reading, simple, instructional guide to leaders and helps people who are working together to build the Church.

Charging the Year 2000

This book will remind you of the last-days' promises of God as well as alert you to the many snares and falsehoods with which Satan will try to deceive and seduce last-days' believers. "A handbook for living in the '90s."

Enduring Hardness

God has called His Church an army and the believers, soldiers. It is mandatory that all Christians endure hardness as good soldiers of Jesus Christ. This book will help build more backbone in you.

How to Avoid Shipwreck

A book of preventive medicine, helping people stay strong and full of faith. You will be strengthened by this book as you learn how to anchor your soul.

How to Relate to Your Pastor

It is very important in these last days that God's people understand the office of pastor. As we put into practice these principles, the Church will grow in numbers and also increase its vision for the world.

How to Always Reap a Harvest

In this book Brother Barclay explains the principles that make believers successful and fruitful. It shows you how to live a better life and become far more productive and enjoy a full harvest.

Improving Your Performance

Every Christian everywhere needs to read this book. Even leaders will be challenged by this writing. It will help tremendously in the organization and unity of your ministry and working force.

The Making of a Man of God

In this book you'll find some of the greatest, yet simplest, insights to becoming a man or woman of God and to launching your ministry with accuracy and credibility. The longevity of your ministry will be enhanced by the truths herein. You will learn the difference between being a convert, an epistle, a disciple, and a minister.

Preachers of Righteousness

This is not a book for pulpiteers or reverends only but for all of us. It reveals the real ministry style of Jesus Christ and the sold-out commitment of His followers—the most powerful, awesome force on the face of the earth.

The Real Truth About Tithing

With the extremely fast lifestyles of these last days, it leaves little time to thoroughly study God's Word. When you finish this book, you will be fully equipped and informed to tithe properly and accurately. All of your tithing questions should be answered. Your life will never be the same.

The Remnant Church

God has always had a people and will always have a people. Brother Barclay speaks of the upcoming revival and how we can be those who are alive and remain when our Master returns.

Sheep, Goats, Wolves

A scriptural yet practical explanation of human behavior in our local churches and how church leaders and members can deal with each other. You will especially enjoy the tests that are in the back of this book.

The Sin of Lawlessness

Lawlessness always challenges authority and ultimately is designed to hurt people. This book will convict those who are in lawlessness and warn those who could be future victims. It will help your life and straighten your walk with Him.

Basic Christian Handbook (minibook)

This book contains basic doctrines that are simple yet necessary to every Christian's walk with God. It will be a vital help to new converts in the Kingdom. This also makes a great tract or altar counselor's tool.

The Captain's Mantle (minibook)

Something happened in the cave Adullum. Find out how 400 distressed, indebted, and discontented men came out of that cave as one of the most awesome armies in history.